To Skye,

Thank you so much
for buying the words of
16 year old me♡

your support means the
world to me♡

Stay magical ✨

Love,

Gabby♡x

This is my story;
Pen to Paper

By Gabrielle Thompson

Acknowledgements

Thank you to my life advisers who have supported me through anything and everything: My Dad; Anthony Thompson. My Teachers/Mentors; Mr. Shaw and Mr. Walton. Also thank you to my family and friends who have also been a great support.

Foreword

This book is a collection of poems and prose that I have written throughout the years. I started writing this poetry around 13/14 years old about things I saw or thought about. Though I feel it is important to add that many of these poems are not my own experiences and that many of them are fictional. A lot of these poems are dark and touch on sensitive subjects but to me they explore the real reality of life. This book serves to tell the stories of others that have not yet found their voice, to tell their story and let their voice be heard. I hope that this book can give people comfort when they feel they are not understood or seen, bring awareness to mental health and other matters that are discussed through the poems and prose. This book may be triggering and that is understandable given the dark nature of it so here is a list of websites you can visit or people you can talk to if you ever need help:

- Childline

www.childline.org.uk

0800 1111

- Samaritans

www.samaritans.org

0330 0945717

- Rape Crisis

www.Rapecrisis.org.uk

- Anxiety UK

www.anxietyuk.org.uk

03444 775 774

- Bipolar UK

www.bipolar.org.uk

- Men's health forum

www.menshealthforum.org.uk

- Mental Health Foundation

www.mentalhealthfoundation.org.uk

- Mind

www.mind.org.uk 0300 123 3393

Contact

For business enquiries:

gabbythompson2919@hotmail.com

Instagram: @gabbythompsonxx

The world will blow out

People are like lightbulbs.
Some brighter than others, some are like
the afterglow just after you turn the light off,
and some are completely broken.
By broken I mean smashed or blown out,
like there is no way they can be fixed or it is
too late.
You never really care about a bulb slowly
dying until it does.
Some bulbs glow all through the day and
when they are alone, they fade out.
Then on the other hand, some glow on their
own.
I think if you saw the world from outer
space, you would be surprised as to how
many bulbs have obliterated themselves.
BANG! And then it's all over.
Never ever lose your shine, even if it is just
a glow, let that light burst and then maybes
the world will gradually become a brighter
place.

Happiness can be found in the darkest of places; you just have to remember to turn on the light.

Bonded by the soul

Those who suffer together have a bond so great, they are bound together for life by their pain; that bond is greater than any bond of love.

2am burnt out fire

It's weird how at night everything hurts more, isn't it?
Your thoughts come alive just like a monster shows its true self at the sight of the moon. Flashes; of everyone that ever hurt you or abandoned you creep into your mind. You sit there and wonder `Why me?' , But then you realize there is something killing everybody, so you have no room to complain.
In the grand scheme of things your problems don't really matter.
But the thing is…they do matter. They do. If they matter to you then that is important isn't it?
The thoughts maul you like a rabid dog. No matter what you do to take the pain away, it will never change the situation. You could run away but what is the use? Changing the scenery does not change the scenario.

The thing about life is, no matter how old you are, whether you're bright or not as smart or even whether you're a girl or boy; it always hurts.

When you lose something that you love or perhaps yourself, it doesn't matter whether you're 13,30 or 80, it's going to hurt you for the rest of your life. No matter how many new looks you try or how many times you dye your hair or how much vodka you drink with your friends, you will still go to bed every night and over analyse every little detail and wonder where the hell you went wrong. You will question why in that brief period of time you allowed yourself to feel happy.

In the blink of an eye you could lose everything.
One day you could get hit by a bus.
The most haunting thought is,
you don't know when that bus is coming or who could be driving it.

Life hurts but you have to choose when you're going to let it hurt you.

You will meet new people who will make you feel like living again. Make you feel worthwhile. The seeds of your soul will grow and blossom again. They may wilter but you can't ever let them die. In the mist of smoke there is light, just sometimes you have to hunt for it; and when you find it, treasure it. In a few years' time the problems you are facing will seem like small battles compared to the war you will win.

The monsters are only out at night, don't let them drag you under.

Please don't let me go bad again.

One of the worst feelings is when you feel yourself going bad again.
You no longer want to smile at strangers or have meaningful conversations on the train.
You dress in all black almost as if to display the darkness that is enclosing you; so much darkness.
You no longer see the world as a place of miracles, instead you see it as a place of misery and despair; the world is making you go bad again.

So, tell me, how do you treat her?

Tell me, how do you treat her?
Do you ignore her the way you do to me?
Do you make her feel like you pain is her
fault?
Do you at least make her feel good enough
for you? Make her feel like you actually give
a shit?
So, go on, tell me! How do you treat her?

Generational trauma

Broken parents break their children in more
ways than they will ever care to know.

I am telling you this because I am going to kill myself

I am going to kill myself.
I am telling you this now so you can start telling people how close we were.
So, you can tell people you never saw the cuts on my wrists and had no idea I was feeling like this and how you wished you could have helped.
I'm telling you this so you can come to my funeral and tell people how I will be deeply missed.
And for the others, I'm telling you this so you can call me selfish and ask others how my family are coping with such a tragedy brought upon their household. So, you can tell people I've wasted my life and I am weak.
For the rest of you, I am telling you this now so you can start telling people how nice I was and how I suffered beautifully for so long. So, you can post the one photo you

have with me captioning it "I hope you're doing okay up in Heaven, we miss you". I am telling you this now to help you because you didn't help me.

Don't do that

Making someone with a mental illness beg for your attention is the worst thing you can do.

Yet again

Here I am on my own crying again after you promised I'd never have to cry on my own again.

It's okay.

You are going to miss a couple of golden hours; you won't be able to go to every party and see everyone that you wish to.
You won't always get to sit in the hustle and bustle of every coffee shop or see every faraway land.
Not everything can be experienced in one life and that is okay.

In my thoughts

Have you ever thought about dying? And I
mean really thought about it.
Have you ever wondered who would
actually care if you died? I mean no one
cares at 4am when you have blood gushing
out of your skin, no one cares when you're
screaming at the top of your lungs because
nothing is ever how it should be even
though it felt so right. Why? Why does no
one ever question anything? Like why
you've had no sleep or why you never show
your arms or why in fact you are so thin?
Why does no one ever wonder and question
these things?
Because they don't care. It's just that
simple.
Why should they care that you tear your
own skin open because it's so hard to live
in? You're the one that does it, don't you?
Have you ever wondered how and why you
are being controlled by a tiny, shiny, piece
of metal? Why does no one ever notice the

adrenaline rush you get at the sight of a pencil sharpener?

Why should they notice that you're falling back into that dark hole again? Why should they notice the red eyes, puffy face and scratched skin?

Why should they notice the anger and the hate that is forced back into your skin like a poison dart?

So, have you ever thought about how you would do it? A gun? A rope? Pills? Or even drowning?

Have you ever thought about what you would say if it failed? What would you tell your family? They would be surprised because just like the rest they haven't noticed anything either.

What would the people you know think? They would probably pretend to be your best friend to get that extra bit of attention you probably need.

Have you ever thought about all of this?

I wouldn't listen to people when they tell you that they are there for you and they notice these things, because they don't. People god damn lie.

If it wasn't for the darkness

If it wasn't for the darkness, I would never have witnessed the morning sky rising, even if it was through blurry eyes.
I wouldn't have known how comforting the ocean can be when you're all alone and insomnia is kissing you goodnight.
If it wasn't for the darkness, I wouldn't have known how beautiful the moon is, even though my lungs were collapsing and my heart was breaking.
I would not have known how precious the light is and for that I am thankful for the darkness.

Those unexpected people

It's horrible being alone, isn't it? Not the sort of alone where you feel a little bit lonely watching people laugh together on the bus, but the lonely where if you died, not a soul would care.

But then the most unexpected person comes along and at first, it's a short breath of fresh air and then over time they fill your lungs.

You learn to breathe again and you no longer feel lonely, you can laugh with those people on the bus.

You breathe that fresh, crisp air and realise there are good people still left in the world and you are cared for.

It's crazy how people like this will impact your life in the biggest ways and they may never know just how much their stupid jokes gradually changed you.

These types of people will always be a part of you within every new breath you take.

These are the sort of people that are worth living for.

Why did you break me like you did?

Why did you have to do that?
Why did you give her all of your attention?
Why wasn't I enough?
Now I can't stop staring at every single
photo of her, trying to pull apart what you
saw in her that you didn't in me.
Why have you made me insecure?
Why have you broken me?

Don't bother

Don't say "does he not realise what's right in front of him?", it does not make me feel better and we all know that if you were him you would do the exact same thing.

You ruined us

What hurt the most wasn't the infidelity
itself, it's the fact I thought you would never
be him.
You weren't supposed to be him, you
promised you wouldn't be him.
Why did you become him?
You ruined us.

Things fall apart

It gets to a point where you go to bed angry at each other even though you both have that fear one of you may not wake up, it just isn't enough anymore. You stop arguing back and instead just take it because you just don't have the fight in you anymore. Or maybes you have just given up.

From there you spend more time alone watching other couples laughing and smiling together and you just sit there reminiscing bitterly.

Before you know it, you are just strangers who share a bed filled with memories of the happier times.

It started with going to bed angry and ended with going to bed wondering at which point everything fell apart.

I was nothing but a coat to you

I was nothing but a coat to you.
I was there to keep you warm in the coldest
of times; even when you wanted just that
little extra heat to get you by.
Once you were warm enough or you wanted
a new design to match your current taste,
you chucked me.
You chucked me, just like you did with the
rest of them. All stacked up in a cold, dark
closet ready for when you needed the warm,
you'd get from me.
But how can I leave when you wrapped me
so tight which made me feel warm too?
Just like a coat I had a purpose.
I was nothing but a coat to you.
Nothing but bits of thread here and there,
tied together using the best parts to make
sure I was just right for you,
Now, I want you to feel the cold, just like the
rest of us, frozen in time.
I was nothing but a coat to you.

Poison tongues

You and I are not defined by the cruel words of others.

Out of place

It is not uncommon to feel like an orphan in a house full of family and a room full of people; your family isn't always your blood.

The difference

He broke my heart into a million pieces.
And then you came along and piece by
piece you picked it up.
You treasured every single piece; you made
my heart a puzzle.
A puzzle that you were going to fix.
Not once did you drop a piece.
You turned the bruises into stains of your
kisses, the cuts, the tears, the anger and the
pain into something so much more beautiful.
You made every broken piece feel fixable.
With you, the moon seemed so beautiful like
it was glowing radiant happiness.
With him, the moon comforted me in the
early hours when I was crying so hard that
my lungs gave out. The air was just so hard
to breathe with him.
He destroyed every aspect of my life,
chapter by chapter, but you embraced every
torn page, no matter how deep it gave you
paper cuts.
You stayed and opened every closed door.

You helped me turn my life around.

It's a cycle

Sometime you are just stuck in a rut, like being stuck in the mud.
You can't move but you can't stop moving,
Happy but deeply dissatisfied,
Motivated and full of ideas but unmotivated to start,
Half way in the mud and half way out,
Then all of a sudden, something excited you and you're right back where you are meant to be.

Introvert

I often feel lonelier in crowds of people than
I do alone.

Rising through the abyss

It is one of the most beautiful feelings when you finally rise out of that abyss of darkness after thinking for so long that you would be stuck there forever.

Because of you

I have learnt to take care of myself because
you did not.
I am swallowed whole by a void knowing
that things should not be this way.

Nothing lasts forever

They say nothing lasts forever.
That means happiness is temporary as is
the sadness.
I think you choose what you want to last in
life.
You can end your sadness and begin your
happiness.
You can choose whether to make your love
last or whether it is going to end in flames.
It is your choice.
Don't let people tell you nothing lasts
forever, because those people once had
something so precious and special to them
that they thought it would last forever but it
didn't.

The signs of suicide

I gave you all my pearls and you said it was
a lovely gesture.
I cut and dyed my hair and you said the
colour suited me.
I started wearing long sleeves and you said
you liked the change of style.
I showed you my poems about suicide and
you said they were good.
I stopped talking and you didn't say
anything.

All the signs were there.
Like red flashing lights warning you
something bad was going to happen.
I gave you all the signs and you gave me
nothing.

As the seasons change
SAD

As the leaves change as do I.
The bright coloured nail varnish turns into a deep black.
The glittering eyes turn to dark, dazed circles, filled to the brim with despair.
The sweet scents of the latest perfumes turn to stenches of stale tobacco and cold coffee.
Floral dresses to long sleeved, black, unwashed shirts.
As the nights grow darker as do I.
No more laughter, just fake smiles.
The talks about our lives will soon stopped and will be replaced by deafening silences.
Coffee dates will be no longer but drinking dates will arise, however I will be alone.
Downing drink after drink until the pain is numbed.

Autumn to winter.
Smiles to sadness.

Mania: What it's like

Some days are bad, these are the days that if you saw me, you would probably think I was insane.
On these I can both cry and laugh in a split second.
Some days are worse.
On these days I drop the fake smile and whisper to myself
I can't do this anymore
These days are the worst, I can't breathe, move or talk.
I am paralysed.
There is only one answer to my problems on these days and that is dying.
I feel like everyone in the world wants to push me over the edge and watch me fall.

Sometimes I'm excited about everything, like nothing in the world matters or is going to stop me.
The world pulls me into a warm embrace.

Sometimes I stay like this for a while but then sometimes I come crashing down, I think I've hit rock bottom and then the floor gives way.
Then, because of the change of mood that is faster than the speed of light, I have episodes.
Episodes where I don't know what is going on or how I'm feeling or who I really am.
When these episodes get bad, I can sometimes see things that other people can't, things that aren't there.

Some months of the year are worse than others.
But I can live with it, can't I?
Some Days I can and some days I can't, that is just bipolar.

Broken

I no longer care.
I think I might have given up.

You can cross that bridge

There is nothing but a single bridge between life and death; one bridge and one decision. One bridge between a new beginning and a certain ending, an ending that should not happen.
Take a step back and take a new road, new path, a new life.
Don't let that bridge be where it all ends, cross that bridge and keep walking, walk until the sun rises again and I promise you, you will end up right where you are meant to be.
Cross that bridge.

Abuse

From a young age we are taught to take a man's nonsense.
What was that quote again?
The one who's pigtails he pulls is the one he loves the most.
Well, he hit me today so he must really love me.
Last week he left a few bruises but that is only because he cares.
Sometimes I do wish he didn't pull my pigtails…
I don't feel loved.

Concealed

I can't tell you how many times I have cried until my eyes were dry,
Hid the stains with some cheap concealer and moved on.
Not once did anyone question, I know they saw the concealer, I know they saw the streaks but as long as I looked okay then that was enough.

Abandoned

There was a hole in my heart that needed
filling,
I thought you were the one to fill it
but instead you just broke more of it away.

I wish my pain was visible

Sometimes I wish you'd hit me so that way the pain is visible,
That way I wouldn't have to question if I was really suffering because the answer would be right there written on my skin; in dark purple and green ink.
If you hit me then I'd know how you really felt, I would see clearly how you feel rather than sitting in the bath crying at 2pm in the afternoon convincing myself that you didn't mean what you said and that you were just angry.
If my scars were visible people would know that you hurt me,
They would tell me to run as fast as I can.
But my scars aren't visible and that is all a part of your trick.

It is not easy to just get over it

People tell you different ways to get over life
and misery,
Have a shower to wash away the day they
say,
But they don't know how the water runs red
and just reminds you of the failure you've
become.
Have an early night it will help to think more
clearly,
They don't see the dark figures that lurk in
the corner of the room that swarm your mind
with thoughts that are darker than the
depths of the ocean.
Look upwards and forwards,
They don't know what it is like to look at the
sky and only see a different world; a world
after life that offers light.
People don't understand that some things
are just too hard to *just* get over.

Neglected

People only see the parts of you they want to see.
You see all the parts.
Every broken part.
The parts that become neglected you become to hate.
You learn to hate yourself because of your anger, no one else wants to see your pain and anger so why should you?
They only want to see your happiness and laughter.
You become this broken jigsaw and you have no idea where the pieces should fit together.
Other people see the complete, perfect jigsaw that they want to see.

Start a riot

Write your poetry, speak your story, sing
your songs.
Shout it from the rooftops until your lungs
shake; it needs to be heard.
It's god damn revolutionary.

Forever scars

All of those god damn years of abuse and all of the god damn nightmares were not enough because here I am still bleeding from the wound you tore open so many god damn years ago.

Intentions

The scariest thing about someone new is
you will never know their intentions.
To them you could just be a passing moon
but to you they could be your total eclipse.
That is scary.
You could meet someone and you may feel
like they are just a branch,
A falling leaf
To them, you could be their whole tree
within a beautiful landscape.
That is the torturous thing about meeting
new people,
Trying to work out their intentions.

She didn't want to turn another page

She looked for friends and lovers in her
books,
But as soon as that chapter ended and
another did not begin,
She was lonely again.

Give yourself time

Give yourself time.
Give yourself time to heal the wounds that
they so viciously ripped open.
Give yourself time for the tears to dry that so
despairingly stained your cheeks.
Give yourself time to become one and
whole again after you were split in two.
It took years for them to break you as hard
as they did so give yourself the time to
rebuild yourself.

I was not always this bitter;
I'm sorry

I wasn't always this bitter,
But now when I see love I can taste the sour on my tongue like off milk,
When I feel love I can feel the venom storming through my veins.
The bitterness and hate invades my heart, almost as if an army has marched inside of me and is ready for war.
You soured my soul.
I once often looked at lovers in awe of their passion,
But now;
I look and I feel disgusted, I feel like telling them that it will not last and that love is not real.
I want to shout and scream while I am sitting on the train watching couples smiling into each other's eyes, I want to tell them that they need to run as fast as they can because he will pull out your roots so you can no longer grow and blossom.

You have made me want to do that,
You have made me bitter,
I am bitter for you.

Greta

So many children speak the truth that adults are just not willing to hear yet.

Please don't

Please do not tell me I have put weight on
and that I am looking healthier,
I know you are being nice but I do not want
that.
I want to be able to see my ribs caressing
my flesh,
I want to be able to see my heart pounding
through my skin.
So, please do not tell me I am getting better;
That is what you want. Not me.

A sea of faces yet I don't know a single one

I surround myself with empty and broken
faces to drown out the loneliness you left
me with.
The loneliest people are often surrounded
by the most.

Gatsby

Gatsby filled his empty halls with empty souls in hopes of being reunited with the one who broke him the most.

She was wrong

She died thinking no one loved her.
She was wrong.

Weighted

My life is like a scale,
That I just can't balance.

Pages of my pain

I spread my feelings across these
notebooks
hoping that the words lift up out of the page
and you hear the voice that is the screaming
inside.

I don't want him

Your colours began to fade as his grew,
And slowly but surely you became him.

Love was ruined for me

I don't know whether it was the crying of my
mother after another man walked out on
her, or the bitterness of my father because
of the betrayal that made me skeptical about
love.
It could have been all the men I was
surrounded by at such a fragile age that
cared for nothing but their own satisfaction;
Or it could have been the times that my
father swore he would never open up to
anyone again.
Whatever it was that tainted love for me has
affected me forever,
I don't want to be like my mother who is so
lonely she looks for nothing but love; I don't
want to be like my father who is so broken
by a Judas kiss he never will trust anybody
again.
Instead, I live my life dodging the arrows of
Cupid so that way I can never be hurt or let
down; if an arrow hits me and pierces my

heart I walk in the shadows where my
insecurities cannot be seen.
I will not allow myself to put my life into a
single soul only for mine to be ripped away
and torn to shreds; I tiptoe around love
almost like a beautiful dance, twisting and
turning away from those I shouldn't.
Love was ruined for me;
I never thought of love as red roses and
star-lit kisses,
For me it was pain and misery,
I will not allow myself to be broken by love
as those around me have been.

Ignorance is not bliss

Whales often beach themselves in order to
die,
Ducks and dolphins drown themselves to
escape the cruel world,
Dogs will starve themselves because of
neglect,
Bears will deny themselves water as an
escape from their captivity,
Insects will self-destruct to protect their
family and loved ones.
Whenever an animal dies from suicide the
world stands with them,
But when a person kills themselves, they
are labelled weak.
Suicide is denied as a problem,
But tell me why when an animal takes their
life it *is* a problem?
We are all part of nature, aren't we?
Suicide is a problem.
A problem throughout nature which shows
the world is not working the way it should
be.

Nature is real; suicide is real.

I've been that girl

I've been the girl who sits at the back of the class with glazed eyes and barely utters a sound, I know her well and she has been through a lot.

I've been the girl who seems like she has got her life in a tight grip with all the best grades and all the right friends, I know that her smile is fake.

I've been the girl who goes to all of the parties and wears all the newest fashions, I know that she goes home every night and cries in her bed.

I've been the girl who is so filled with anger that she cannot allow herself to feel happy; only bitterness, well I know her too and I know that there is a broken girl behind all of that venom.

I know all of these girls; I've been all of these girls and I know that life had broken them so they continued to break themselves.

All of these girls have stories, all different
but the pain hurts the same;
Never judge a girl by her cover.

Please don't remind me

The rubbing of my jeans against my broken skin is a constant reminder that I broke a promise to myself.
The stinging in the shower as the water pours through my open wounds is nothing compared to the pain, I have caused other people.
The faded lines and scars are a memorial to the happy girl I once was.
So please don't remind me that I messed up.
Don't remind me that I killed your happiness with the right move from a sharp edge.
Don't remind me that I used to be a better person and that you would give anything to get her back.
Just don't remind me because I already know.

Destruction

Clattering, shaking,
Crying and breaking.

The Darkest hour

The darkest hour is not just when you're standing on the edge of that cliff, thoughts swarming your mind while you decide whether to take the last step to end it.
The darkest hour can be while you are out late afternoon with your friends,
Pretending to listen to their joyful conversations; while you are sat there drinking drink after drink wondering how they ended up so happy and why you didn't.
It can be 4am when you're lying on your bed, screaming into your pillow asking why that man had to abuse his power to tear you in half. *Literally.*
The darkest hour does not just have to be when you are at breaking point;
It can creep up on you at any moment, the light fades and the moon rises differently for everyone.

I live in a dollhouse

I live in a dollhouse.
I am dressed up as the person you want me to be to please your crowd,
You tear apart my stories as if they mean nothing and only dare to say the parts that will suit their taste.
To all of your people I am a knight in shining armor to suit the situation,
But to you I am nothing but a doll,
No one will ever know who I really am or who you really are,
Everyone is blind to what really goes on when the lights are turned off and the doors are locked, they are too distracted by your flattering personality and expensive jewelry.
They will never see how broken you are and how you fill the emptiness inside of you with drinks and men.
If only they turned on the lights,
They would see the real show without the makeup and the props,

The fancy jewelry, the expensive drinks, the perfect children and of course the well paying job.

If they tore down the walls of this dollhouse, they would find the broken home that you so desperately try to hide.

This is no dollhouse; this is my life.

I don't want to

I think that one of the hardest things is forcing yourself to let go of someone you never thought you would.
I thought you would always be there,
But now it's nothing but the shadow of your love that follows me.
You were supposed to be there forever, this isn't how it is meant to be, but you found a new life.
A life I wasn't apart of and god dammit I wanted to be a part of that life; I still want to be a part of it more than anything.
But you don't want that otherwise you would have called,
So now it is time to let go and that is something I never thought I would have to do with you.

The hardest part: rebuilding a home

I thought the hardest part would be leaving the home that we spent countless hours building together.
Leaving the happiness we had created in each other's presence, all the shades of yellow and orange chosen especially for our little piece of Heaven; but that wasn't the hardest part.
The hardest part was not leaving.
The hardest part was trying to build a home with someone else that was not you.
Trying to forget that the locks do not always mean control, they can mean safety.
It was hard to look at the vases in the middle of the room without flinching in fear; that they would be thrown off the yellow wall that was supposed to show our happiness.
The vases in our home had beautiful roses in them; I wish I saw the thorns before it was too late, now all I see is the thorns.
I wish I saw the thorns, the locks on all the doors and most of all I wish I saw the fence

that kept me hostage in what was supposed
to be our home.
The hardest part was not leaving our home;
it was trying to forget you in a new one.

The ripple effect

One moment in your life can make that much of a splash that it ripples on throughout your life,
It changes everything,
Years later you find yourself still reflecting on that one moment and wonder will it ever leave you? Would your life be different?
Ripples just continue to grow until they disappear much like moments;
Sometimes they become so big it is overwhelming and you can't breathe but sometimes they just don't last long enough.
I call this the *ripple effect.*

You do you

Do whatever it is you have to do to get you through.

Healing is not always beautiful

Let yourself heal, do yoga, cry for days in bed, scream and shout at the moon, write your poems and don't be afraid to speak them.
Do whatever you have to do to heal and remember that it isn't always beautiful.

Losing you

It was like falling off the edge of a cliff,
And looking up to see you with a blank face
and a hand that was not out to catch mine.

How I knew I had fallen out of love

I knew I had fallen out of love when the moon started becoming my friend again in the early hours of the morning when I was crying out of loneliness; and when I started dreading the sun rising because it meant a new day was starting.
I knew I had fallen out of love when the butterflies in my stomach turned into stinging bees; and the sweet taste in my mouth turned sour.
I knew I had fallen out of love but I wouldn't tell you.
I wouldn't tell you because I knew you hadn't,
I knew you still smelt the roses and tasted the honey.
I fell out of love but you didn't.

I stayed with you; but I didn't love you

I stayed with you because I needed to feel loved.
I needed to fill the emptiness that was inside of me;
I hoped you would fill the void.
I stayed as long as I could,
Still feeling a hole;
Like a part of me was missing.
Then I realised I needed to love myself to fill the space that took up so much room.
That is why I stayed,
That is why I stayed with someone I did not love.

The tortured poet

Isn't it sick how I get inspiration from my
pain?
The suffering of others,
The mess of the world.
It's quite depressing concept really; the
tortured poet.

Please turn the light on

It's like waking up in the middle of the night and even though my eyes are wide open it's all still dark; that is what it feels like to lose you.

The picture in our heads will ruin us one day

Don't have expectations for anything because the picture in your head will ruin everything.

<u>Feeling something is better than nothing at all</u>

I can feel the distance between us,
The air is thicker than it was before,
You don't look at me like you used to; in
fact, you don't look at me at all.
I try to close the gap,
Make the air thinner
But I see that it is too late.
There is no distance between us;
There is nothing.

Whatever happened to my destiny?

I always thought I'd be destined for great things; yet I feel invisible in a crowd of people that have done nothing but great things.

Addicted to the pain

Why did you stay so long?
Why did you leave rehab?
Why did you carry on that way?
They ask.
The pain and suffering brought me comfort,
it's all I've ever known.
Sometimes I miss the sadness.

The eyes will always tell the story

I look at her with tear and fire filled eyes,
I see your eyes when you look at her,
I see the lust and the desire,
I can't compete with her as for in your eyes
she is perfect.

I see that now

I see you delete her name from your phone,
I see the way you don't love me like you
used to,
But most of all,
I see that I am no longer good enough for
you,
I see that now.

A dichotomy

You don't understand me and you never will; that is both your blessing and your curse.

Don't give me things to write about

You tell me that you hate it when I write
poems about you,
This whole time I've been writing poems
you're out there saying and doing things for
me to write about.
Look at what I'm trying to tell you.

During Covid-19

Don't let others make difficult times even more difficult for you.

Isolated

You push me away and tell me to go and
see other people,
Yet I look around and see no one but you.

Today's society

Sometimes you can do all of the right things
and still feel deeply unhappy.
The problem is not you my dear; it's the rest
of the world.

It's never just okay

They say that it is the calm before the storm,
but then they also say that after the rain
there will be a rainbow, so which one is it?
I've learned that life will never settle, it's
never just okay, life is never grey.
It's for you to choose which problems you
give your energy to.

Marty

Stay cool baby.

This is my story now

This is my story now.
No matter how many faces I want to drift
away,
No matter how many sights I wish I could
remove from my mind's eye,
This is my story now.
No matter how many times I wish I could
start a new life,
Just move away and start over,
I can't.
The past will always be there,
No amount of new faces could replace the
ones already known,
No amount of words that speak love will
replace those that spit venom.
This is my story now.

After everything

And then after that,
I never looked at the sky the same way
again.

About the author

Hi! Thank you for choosing this book and making the time to give it a read. I really hope that it helped you in some way and I would love to hear how this book helped you through instagram or twitter! So, a little bit about me (I have no idea what to write I just know that the real authors do a section like this at the end of their book!). At the time of writing this I am a 20 year old girl living in the UK, I'm studying at university while working in a restaurant and running a tarot reading facebook page (I like to keep busy). I'm studying to become a life coach or a therapist since my one true passion is helping people. As of right now, I am working on another poetry and prose book all about witchcraft, spirituality and healing! Over the past few years spirituality, witchcraft and alternative healing have helped me greatly and since I also love to write poetry I'm trying to put the two together! If you want to find out more about me or you are interested in my current ventures such as my tarot reading business you can find me on instagram @gabbythompsonxx. I hope this book finds you well and I promise that if you are going through anything that it will get better!

Be sure to leave me an amazon review and I'll see you soon!

Love,
Gabby x

I thank you for your support.

Printed in Great Britain
by Amazon